Somewhe Pale Blue Dot

Written by:

Afsoun Zarrin,

James Goff, &

Matthew Principe

Edited by:
James Goff

Off-Kilter Publishing

Somewhere on a Pale Blue Dot

Written by Afsoun Zarrin,
James Goff, & Matthew Principe

Edited by James Goff

First Edition Published
Montrose, PA - Mar. 2021
Off-Kilter Publishing

ISBN: 979-8-675-91550-7

Dramatized for cathartic purposes.

For more info, please visit
OffKilterPublishing.com

Contact the publisher at
OffKilterPub@protonmail.com

For the Lost Ones,

And the Found Ones

Table of Contents

Somewhere

on a

Pale

Blue Dot

Written by:
**Afsoun Zarrin,
James Goff,
Matthew Principe**

Water

"Swimming is a confusing sport, because sometimes you do it for fun, and other times you do it to not die. And when I'm swimming, sometimes I'm not sure which one it is."

- **Demetri Martin**, "Why Swimming is a Confusing Sport," *Comedy Central Presents: Demetri Martin*, 3/19/2004

A Drop of Water

Oh,
to be
A Dro p
o f Wate r,

The very thing that brought this all.

Coalescing into Rivers,
Rushing through lush rainforests,
Carving the cliffside of paradise,
Stretching on into Forever.

O h , t o b e
a D r o p o f W a t e r,

Immaterialized in the Clouds,
Looking down upon the Earth–
Til suddenly, so quickly, falling,
Diving, racing, chasing it's way
To meet a billion racing brothers.

be a
h, to   Dr
O   op
of
,retaW
In the washing machine of this World.

JG

Cold Erosion

Waves of mutation,
Force divides.

All good things
Once were mine.

This cold erosion
Means more inside.

Lay down.

This story's broken down, pushed aside.
Thought crimes deplete the mind.
A soul's devotion caught beside a spine
That cries for more next time;
An old commotion for my softer side.

MP

Silence Passed

Why do I keep speaking
    When no one is listening?
    Staying silent requires discipline,
        But my unheard words just hang–
In dissonance.

        Tearing open new found distances,
    The silent words begin drizzling;
My contributions are now dwindling.
    An unheard storm incoming,
        In a societal world, it's limiting,
But why continue when no one is listening?
    Because silence requires discipline,
        Which falls outside
societal conditioning,
        The speed of which
    just keeps quickening–
The lack of stillness is sickening.
But the words I speak aren't interesting,
So no one is listening,

        Leaving my words to hang–
In dissonance,

Ever expanding the lonely distances.

I spent so many years in silence,
Why can't I find that again?
My voice is in defiance, driving pilot–
I say more than I intend.
My will has no reliance
if the words keep rolling
with no end.

I always sound dumb,
I say too much,
And come across wrong,
using words as my crutch.

I need to shut the fuck up,
and passively sit back,
Let life flow, cut some slack.
For most, silence is the most difficult task,
For a while I had it, but once again
it has passed.

There is nothing more peaceful

than when silence is grasped.

AZ

All Talk

The thunderous cavalry
  Tramples the boastful ambitions
    Of those who swore
      They meant what they said.
Will strong will ever be enough?
        Each contemptuous silence
    Breeds hidden violence.
         Behind your eyelids,
    These traps do lay.
Finding solace in the waves,
   I have done all that I can do.
What's there left to be close to?
  I'll drown in the wake of your light,
Drenched in sour speech.
  You were just another dream
That's better than my life.
  Why can't we see through
      The eye that lies above?

Will we ever meet the young tongue
Of the dawn in the quiet moments
That define our loud actions.

      MP

The World Marches On

Cycles of sadness
Like rain repopulate.
My brain escalates,
The world marches on.

I'm still in bed,
Old habits have returned.
Thoughts start to burn –
And the world marches on.

With close friends,
I hardly speak.
This house is bleak –
I'm barely hanging on.

JG

Inutilia

In boredom I ask: What makes me me?

In search of some sort of meaning.
Of course, I'm dust and other debris.

But what do I bring to society?

Bitter for all the jobs I could hold;
You have such potential! I used to be told.

But with no direction I succumb to mold.
On which path should I walk bold?

At twenty-two, the future is vast,
But with the flags at half mast
I won't escape disappointments of past.
I'd like to do more than simply last.

When I am old, for what will I be proud?
What stories will be told from under my
                                    shroud?
What expressions will lie on the face of the
                                    crowd?
What accolades and cruelty will I allow?

For what will I let myself be loud?

JG

Depression is a Bomb

Depression is a bomb;
In the face of it be calm.
I handle it with aplomb;

I'm fooling everyone but mom.
I stay calm.
Fight my qualms.   I open up my palms
But can't find any psalms for this.
No, I just sit here, reminisce
On the time I could exist
Without being a diss
To this society
That's just a jist.

Depression is a bomb;
In the face of it, be calm.
I handle it with aplomb;

I'm fooling everyone but mom.
The force of it hits strong.   I stay calm.
I open up my palms-
Don't need any psalms.
I'll just sit here,   stay calm,
Bear the force of this here, bomb.
I'll handle it with aplomb.
I'm sorry, Mom.

AZ

Who do I Turn to Now?

Who do I turn to now?
Do I even deserve that?
My parents' hearts aren't around–
They're always mad,
So much on their plates;
I can't make a sound.
Too young to be their therapist,
Too sad to stick around.
They want to chain me by the wrists,
So I try to stay unfound.
A future of success,
But that's what I'm doing now.
And friends? Where are those?
When will they come around?
I lost all the old ones,
No new ones to be found.
I'm close to no one,
And the darkness starts to surround.

The silence takes over,
And in the empty world I drown.
Most consistent were the lovers,
But I burned all those bridges too.
When reality's uncovered,
They never follow through.
I'm in love again,
But that might end too.
And then who's left?
Do I even deserve that?
Should I give my heart a rest,
Or try to fight back?
I'm close to no one,
And the darkness starts to surround.
The silence takes over,
And in the empty world I drown.

AZ

Grey Days

Grey days form a haze.

       I've lit ablaze the last paycheck.

If I think for a second

       Where it has gone,

I'll look at the toilet

       And hope I'm wrong.

A mountain of madness

    Building slowly.

An ocean of comfort

    Faintly glowing.

Grey days form a haze.

       I forgot my glasses,

          Where did you go?

       JG

The Glue Won't Stick

I'm tired of beating all of my shit
 to such states of shit.
Each possession slowly regresses
 to such a state of shit.
My evolved specimen of a body
 degraded to shit.
The innocent baby born
 into a hundred years of shit.

Why does nothing fit?

The glue won't stick.

The painting won't sit.

The mufflers fucked to such a state of shit.

I'm fully aware it is not an option to quit.
Through all the shit I have to stick
This out, release all doubt, show my grit.
 Show my life is more than just a heap of shit,
 That I have what it takes to make this world fit.

JG

Numb

Neutral,
      numb,
            no longer fun.

I lost my beat,

             I'm on the run.

Can't find my feet,

             can't find the sun,

Can't feel the heat,

             my skin is numb.

No more emotions,

             I feel so dumb;

I lose my thoughts,

             they fall to crumbs,

I hate this feeling–

             No longer fun.

             AZ

Writer's Block

Why am I having writer's block?

Are there no more thoughts,
Or are they locked?

Are my emotions out of stock?

Or are my actions stuck?
Time is running round the clock.

The words aren't coming–
Writer's block.

Bullshit, actually.

I am the block,
Cutting off emotional stock;

Holding the thoughts,
But running the clock,

Not producing writing isn't a shock.

AZ

Lost in a Town

Lost in a town
　　　　　Filled with frowns,
　　　　　I look at the ground
　　　　　　　　　.dnuora nrut dnA

I'm lost in this town
　　　　　　　Of suits and gowns.
　　　　　　　You all get around
　　　　　Til you're found out.

Lost in this town
　　　　　Of grey and brown,
　　　　　Won't make a sound,
　　　　　　　For fear they'd drown.

　　　　JG

Winter

Cold ears,

No fear,

You were never someone that I'd know.

The sweetest kill in mystery season –

To see my fate drip,

Into the cold snow..

Bleed me out of me.

As I keep asking the same questions,
I know that I ask the same questions.

Because everyone that answers me lies.

MP

Work

Everybody's doing something,
So let's get up and out of bed.

Everybody keeps progressing,
They push on and on ahead.

If I want to catch up,
If I want to live the dream,

I better get up,

Get to work

Working.

JG

No One

What do you do
When it feels like there's no one?
When Mom's mean too,
Just gotta deal with the outcome.

Who do I turn to,
When all the friends ran, too?
There's drugs on the loose,
They're losing their minds-
Fools.

And no one will move,
Emotions are all gone.
How can they choose
That society's not wrong.
How are they fooled
By the fuel that the government spews?
Why do they choose to disapprove of me,
Leaving me with few to prove
It's worth the move through life,
And choose to live,
Because without love,
Life is nothing,
And without love,
She sits alone,
Questioning her worth.

AZ

Cold

The cold longs to hold me close,
It rips and tears through my clothes.
My blood retreats within my coat,
And I endure another frost.

JG

$5 words

You were a poet,
                    Straight up & down

Integrated apparitions.

I used to think
                    I had to sound

Pretty enough for you to hear me.

It's gluten-free,
                    In case you were wondering,

No need to feel guilty.

Expensive speech   With $5 words

                Never sounded so cheap.

                    MP

Pouring from a Glass Half-Empty

You have the softest shoulders
My eyes have ever felt.
My sock drawers full of singles–
I'm down to my last belt.

Your feet fall so feebly,
Careful as a tiger.
My favorite hat full of holes–
I can't escape the fire.

Though my lonesome heart yearns,
I know I've yet to earn
A love so hot it burns,
And melts my frozen heart.

And so alone I stay,
Seeking rules to obey.
Blinded, I feel my way
Back to an unmade bed.

JG

A Put Out Flame

Mundane

Routine.

Same same,

Never different.

Mundane,
Same same,
Going insane,
Feeling the blame.

I hate playing this game.

Same same,
Mundane,
Nothing ever changes.
With fame and blame,

All playing the game.

Same same,
Mundane,
A lonely world,
A put out Flame.

AZ

Starve the Artist

Rocks, oven, or gun,
What causes us to run?

Drinks, dope, or bong,
How'd we go so wrong?

A candle burnt out,
Fueled by sorrow and doubt.

The road ends in the river–
Those thoughts used to bring shivers.

Any way, any day, it will pass,
And one of these days,

Will be the last.

JG

Why do I Try?

Conflicted bounds bring new sounds
        to my ear;
Why must I be stuck in this place between
        strength and fear?
What might I hold near in a time
        so queer?

I feel entropy spiraling around me,
            as the clouds resemble fire growling.

Why must the air be so thick
                    in the valley of my mind?

Where are the deer & wild horses
                    that gallop so fine?

My will seems to be tested with every try,

                    Does it exist?

                        Do I?

            MP

Lost in a Dream

                I'm lost in a dream–
Mourning the past,
Staying asleep.

A love that slipped fast,
But cut me so deep.
But nothing will last,
If I'm not feeling free.

The weight of the pain
Is crushing on me.
Can't loosen my grip,
I'm falling asleep,
                I'm lost in a dream.

The curse can be flipped
If my soul is cleaned–
My strengths redeemed.
If I slip away free,
              Pull out of this dream.
Wake up from my sleep.

Time to bury the past deep.
Time to take my next leap.

                    AZ

Condemned, We Endure

A lonely task it has come to be,

That with which we are burdened.

Laid down upon the barest shoulders,

A world so heavy and distorted.

Somehow we'll hold until our end.

JG

Earth

"Ah, this is delicious! What is that, bacteria?
Mmm, mmm—Mm! it's so good.
I can feel it wiggling down my windpipe,"

   – **Sean Patton**, on pretending to like kombucha,
Live @ the Apt, 06/03/19

To the Lost Ones

To the lost ones,
The ones that left, and the ones I hurt,
The memories are not gone.
Time is theft, but the times were good at first,
And those times are not lost.

To the lost ones,
It pains me to think of you,
What did I do?
What did you do?
I miss the times of fun.

To the lost ones,
I'm mourning the past,
While the future comes fast–
Emotions are on the run.

To the lost ones,
You weigh heavy on my mind,
You are lost, but there's more to find,
I'm just not the one.

To the lost ones,
The memories are not gone,
Those times are not lost.
Time is theft, but the times were good at first,
And those times are not lost.

To the lost ones,
And the found ones,
Time is temporary,
And then we're gone.

AZ

Roads

A foreseen pipe dream
Starts to gleam in the corner of my eye,

As my heart screams
And mind sings it seems I'll soon find
The open road, all alone.

Worn bones seeking their rebirth,
Not much do I know,
But to go down open roads traversing the
                    Blessed Earth.

JG

Beans

The precious echo of risen voices
Amongst the ring of nature.

A mother's call to join us all
In a realm that we must share.

Leaking noise
In nature's toys
As drops of water drown us.

I want to let the sun kiss me.
I bet he's haunting.

That's why I laugh–
If you look at it closely,
The dragonflies are preparing.

It's those little moments that happen
And then they're gone;
They're like stars exploding.

I can't look at it right now;
My brain is made of orange beans–
I think another bean escaped.

AZ

Patience in Pieces

In visceral disenchantments
Of theological perceptions,
It comes like a wine decanting,
Idealizing morbid escapism,
Drunk on young blood
Walking through unfamiliar forests,
I hear conversations
Of nomadic preservations,
Oh! the humanities,
International starvation
Of patients for peace
Leaves patience in pieces.

MP

Moldy Flower

Moldy flower,
You were born into nature,
Destined to seal the love of two.

Mariage ties in marigold,
Now your skin is full of mold,
Trapped in time,
You lost your gold.

Moldy flower,
Once you held love,
Now you are dry.

All things living are destined to die.

AZ

Friday

It's Friday & I don't want to talk,
As I hear these lectures
peanut
From the   gallery
About their cake walk.

So I'll clean out this trailer–
Don't hand me a mop.

Let the music play,

Thinking about all that happened
To make things this way,
Drink till I'm flagged,
My mind beyond shagged;

My face still stings from that slap.

Just let me be,
Just leave me alone,

We don't need to exchange words
Til insults are thrown,
Sometimes I drive too fast
When I'm alone,
But how would you know?

MP

El Dorado

Have you yet found
Your el Dorado?
The golden city
That holds no knives.
The priestess holding
Flame to page,
Here knowledge dies–
Lost to the ages.

Within you lies
A cornucopia.
Within you lies
Divine utopia.
The only knowledge
None at all.

JG

Circle

Start considering;
Dwell upon a It.
Contention holds civilization at misery—
We gave it up.

Return to primitive conditions.
Contention of civilization,
Facts we seek to protect against the threats
Emanating from a suffering civilization.

Grasp this impediment in dimensions true,
Prevent the circle from closing.
Psychic apparatus in pain—
Course enjoyment.
Circular movement, failing,
Again and again,
To attain the movement—
True drive.

Hazy womb—
Receptacle space—
Rhythm,
Precedes the receptacle,
A space the universe resides.
A space exists always—
destroyed,
fixed,
All things come to be.

AZ

11/18/2020

A fresh layer of snow
Blinds my morning eyes,
And yet I cannot think
Of a more pleasant sight.

The cars inch forward
On roads not yet paved;
The dogs can't help but sprint,
Bounding every which way.

Still it is coming down
In soft, picturesque flakes.
I stare out my window:
What a view this world makes.

JG

Valley of Flowers

I want to take you to the Valley of Flowers,
The rolling hills will make us feel little,
Like beans,
And this beautiful Valley will
Look like a dream scene.
I want to walk with you for hours,
Through the colorful flowers
And watch your movements flow,
Naturally at peace,
As the trees blow a breeze,
And hold us at ease,
In this beautiful Valley,
A dream scene.

AZ

Enter

A complex process at the onset.
Squeaking out nonsense,
Seeking concepts to progress.
Reaching deep,
Til I'm lost in quicksand,
Til supply and demand
Makes the daily plans.
Trying to buy the van
To see the land,
To see who I am,
And see what that means.
To become the man,
To see how I can
Catch grip and stand.
Facing the noise, I rejoice.
Making the choices
To raise the voices
Of the boys and girls
I chase this with.
Racing through mazes,
I'm lost in the pages
Trying to save this bliss.

JG

Times Past

Dear fools,
Lady dazed in aimless ize,
Floating in your blue balloon,
You know she hurts sometimes,
Her light frabjous –
Brighter than the midday sun.
But on other side of mourning,
Who knows who we'll become;
The different realms
Between mind & brain.

We here are,   Wei Wu Wei,

Through glass doors,
A mad stifled witness
Wanders down convoluted paths –
Abandoned in the house of love.

Freak out   Far out   Here now,

In your agreeably green sweater,
With a twenty-dollar bill,
On the way to get your fill.
In those nights you thought
To never see the light of day,
To be a slave to your sweet dismay.
Will this ever fade away?

MP

22

Where is the wine,
The new wine,
Dying on the vine.

Can't seem to find
The fruits of my labor.
Oh! Here, they rot on the table.

For this, surely there's a fable.
It seems to have died,
Within my mind.

JG

Heart Bloom

You are an Earth bean
With a light beam
Sturdy as a tree,
Light like the breeze–
Your movements like water,
Your love like fire,
Your heart is my desire,
Your attention I would die for.
You are an Earth bean;
You are one with nature.
Nature flows through you,
And with you my heart blooms.
My heart belongs to you.
And we belong to nature.
And our love will flow through,
And together we will bloom.

AZ

Signs

The third kind's in the headlines—
Civil war on the front door.

Fragile lives ignore the signs—
I implore, what're we here for?

Ancestors, ancient investors—
What could lie beyond the skyline?

Push farther toward foreign inventors—
Brittle minds ignore the signs.

JG

Poison Tree

I   loved   you,

I   loved   you   with

The   innocence   of   my   being,

With no forgone conclusions or meaning. I

loved you without judgment or doubt, with all

my heart poured out, & I continue to eat

T   h   e   fru   i   t

F   r   om t   h   e

P   o   i   s   onou   s   t   r   e   e.

T   oget   h   e   r

W   e   plan   t   e   d

T   h   e   s   e   e   d
of something you no longer believe.

MP

Back to the Core

Stale summer days
Blown up in haze,
Spent finding ways
To kill the boredom.

At Doug's place again,
Until the day comes
To give in to bends –
Be born again.

A whole new world –
As Aladdin soared.
Go back to the core,
And survive the World.

JG

Seven Sisters Tree

Trees bleed sap,

                    They're freed.

Free from the map,

                    Their seed.

Knees need not flap,

                    They're trees.

Bees on their lap,

                    Do not flee.

Feed the gap,

                    Bleed the map,

We are trees.

                    Be the sap,

Need not flap,

          We are freed.

          AZ

Deficit

Vicious repetition –
Childhood glasses too
scratched to fix my vision.

Internal sedition –
To break these old habits
requires mental fission.

Gross misrepresentation –
Childhood dreams long since shattered,
Struggling to balance the equation.

Unfortunate fortification –
As their helping hands
Save me from starvation –
Hold me in stagnation.

JG

Solace

Contemptuous shadows shout
Tumultuous imprecations
In the changing winds.

An agnostic nature,
Magniloquent circumstances,
Chances squandered
In laughable forlorn aphorisms.

Pondering in her minds tenements,
She runs,
Unable to contextualize tender times.

Novelties sigh.   In eloquent illusions

Perplexed by failed fusion
To celestial soliloquies.

There, you see,
It's only theology.

Holy, she swoons
Into the trees

Behind her eyes   To find solace

In Identity.

MP

Indifference

On the television I watch
The ages of old–
Convoluted memories,
Misguided history.
And I idolize their pain–
The rapturous death of war,
Fought with sword and shield.
Lives ending before ripeness,
Loves lost to loyalty.
Unfettered emotions,
We no longer reach.

I am an average man.
Surely I should have died yet.
But I'm fortunate enough
To live in the days
Of immortality
And indifference.

JG

Green Little Tent

This valley is unimaginably beautiful,
    Lush with shades of green–
Trees and fields, mountains and rivers;
    Our green little tent sits alone
In the vastness of this valley.
    Through the door,
There are layers of mountains to admire.
    The sunset vibrant and slow,
A gift to witness–
    Now the stars shine bright above,
An endless depth into the universe.
    A sky full of stars protects us in this night,
As we are nothing but universe dust,
    With too many thoughts,
        Too little to matter.

AZ

See It All

Oklahoma, Tennessee,
    Oh, the places I could be;
Montana, Arkansas,
    I just wanna see it all.

    Boggling geography
    Up and down the fields and streams,
      So bizarre just how far
My little car will roll to see it all.

Alaska and now down to Maine,
    Could it be that we're the same?
New Mexico, Wyoming,
    I wonder who I can bring.

My brain cannot contain the frames –
Insane, I stare at waving grains.
Mystifications come with the elevation,
Aforementioned distance I swiftly erase.
    Expeditional missions –
    I've gone fishing for a living.
    A spacious place to breathe in –
    The first forgotten season.

JG

Lemon - Limes

Lush little lemon – limes,
Leeching off each other's lines.

Sour tongue, liquid lies,
Laces like your little eyes.

Liquid lines, lick my lies,
Leave it till the liquid dries.

Live in lies, let it die,
Sour tongue, lucid eyes.

Lay awake through passing time,
Let it dry, stay alive.

Lush little lemon – limes,
Leeching off each other's lines.

Sour tongue, liquid lies,
Leave it till the liquid dries.

AZ

Dawn to Dusk

Petulantly he sits,
Waiting for the demise
Of his most recent surprise.
One of shared compromise,
An inception in disguise.
Are his thoughts only lies?
Or is his rational mind
Only seeing what time does to life?

You can see the nausea in his eyes,
& the realization
That what he desperately wishes
won't come true.
Acted out as if manifested
From his own mind.

How much longer will he wait
Til the sun meets the horizon,
Til this sinking feeling
No longer leaves him fleeting
Into himself,
Not sure how to be.
When will things feel right?

MP

I Will See You Soon

Somewhere on a Pale Blue Dot
I sit, thinking of You.
You, temporarily lost,
But I will see You soon.

Somewhere on a Pale Blue Dot
We laughed the Darkness away.
We shared Our intimate thoughts,
And sucked the juice from each day.

Somewhere on a Pale Blue Dot
Spinning around the Universe,
Lives tied in a Cosmic knot,
Where once I was, appeared Us.

Somewhere on a Pale Blue Dot
You tracked down this tired soul.
You gave me Food, a Blanket and, Cot,
Wrapped me up in fur.

Somewhere on a Pale Blue Dot
The threads connect Our lives
And tie Together the lot-
Where once I was, appeared We.

Somewhere on a Pale Blue Dot
I'm sitting thinking of You-
Somewhere out There wondering,
Where I will see You soon.

JG

Fire

"*I came back inside,
and that pot of oil was on fire.
So thinking quickly, with my brain, I thought
'What, historically, is very good at fighting fires?'
And water, **HISTORICALLY**, is a very effective
fire-fighting tool,*"

- **K. Trevor Wilson**, *Winnipeg Comedy Festival, 2016*

Burning Bridges

I burn more bridges than candles these days.
I feel like the scandal,
Catching everyone's dirty gaze.
It's more than I can handle,
So I'm lost in a constant haze.

I've got a plan, though,
But, for now, I'm passing days.
This bubble is a bramble,
And I'm ready to set ablaze.

Dancing fire, like a candle-
For a minute you caught my gaze.
I pulled my hand, though,
And with it I pulled the flame.

Smokey hands hold fallen ash,
A history erased.

It was more than I could handle,
So I knew I had to quit the game.

AZ

Good Morning

What will I do today?
What songs will I play?
Is this the end of days?
When will I go away?

How do I talk to them?
Do I have a best friend?
Just how far can I bend?
Will I ever find the end?

Why is this the way I feel?
Should I get a haircut,
Or will I regret it again?

And will I regret these days?
The old habits that have stayed,
Like me in this bed all day.

JG

Plastered

Propaganda plastered:
Obey thy Master.

Public opinions scatter
While youthful dreams shatter.

Question; Does it really matter?

That at the top of the ladder

There's a bunch of fat cats that slather

Shit to conform to.
Pretending this reality is the norm–

Fool.

Try to pull your thoughts & gather,

While they keep the tensions high.
Don't get lost in chatter–

Have you been borne yet
And are you alive?

MP

Sad Actors

Life has no redeeming factors –
We're all sad actors with nothing to act for.

Losing the cause, failing the facts,
Only ones who survive are the abstractors.

The ones that stay alive,
They thrive off the backs of the malefactors.

Police control and maintain like the reactors,
But this isn't physics, it's not hieroglyphics.

There's injustice and corruption,
Let's get down to the specifics.

Life has no redeeming factors –
We're all sad actors with nothing to act for.

AZ

Leaving Love Behind

Diamond eyes
Hide a sigh–
A subtle sign
Of disappointment.

I leave the drive
On a slow ride,
Leaving love behind–
Feeling discontent.

Oh god why
Did I ride
Away?

JG

Subtleties

You never picked up on the subtle things.

Every excuse used up
Leaves us with no trust,
Entropy around us swirling,
A cool wind we strive to brave,
Trying to remain resilient.

For the moments we spend
Should be honest & true,
Stop nickel & diming your time,
Know what it's like to be
& be treated Kind.

I'll notice the subtle differences
That make us who we are,
Wondering how long we are going
To continue this method acting.

Pretending to be the people we're not,
Although I can't hear your words,
I can feel the pain you mean to inflict.

MP

Arguments of Nonsense

We've made murderers out of madmen,
Corpses out of sad men,

Where is our humanity?

We've formed arguments of nonsense,
By now Einstein would say amen.

JG

A Love Willing to Bend

I'll put my love on the line-
All the thoughts crossing my mind.
The single love yet to die.
The single love I've yet to find.
What connection is yet to end?
What love willing to bend?
It's to you I send
These broken thoughts,
Trying to mend
A love I fled.
Hidden inside,
I leave signs.
On meager morsels,
I will fend.
I'll put my love on the line
For a love willing to bend.
The single love I've yet to find
When broken thoughts are brought to mend.

JG

Noise Pollution

Noise pollution. Nationalism. Narcissism.
How much space does your noise take up?

Were you taught it,

did you take it,

was it taken?

Can money reserve all of this space
to be filled with sound?
Or do you make the sound and fill the space
at the hands of your ego's boundaries?
Who taught you to take with no regard?

The vastness of the sky

can be bought by no one,

And yet your sounds echo-

Tearing apart the sky,
for distances beyond the eye.
And water, so sensitive and vulnerable,
Forced to carry the rolling echo
of your noise pollution.
Do you see? This time it is a pie.
When you take, you are taking
from an unreplenishable source.
When you take, you are directly taking
from others.
If you take too much, you silence
everyone else.

So why America?

Why must you pollute
the entire night sky
with shattering sounds of terror?
Is it to celebrate, or convince us
that you won the pissing contest with Britain
over a pre-existing nation you shat upon?
The audacity to celebrate this
as an independence like you're the victims
and the victors, and not just a new strain
of colonizers that came to oppress
and destroy a richly cultured people.
Power hungry and narcissistic,
America, you may be independent,
But you're no different.

AZ

Dial tone

With 3 shots and 2 to the head

I knew justice had been avenged.

The quiet evening brought me now to rest.

It didn't help that you,

A sweet little thing,

Couldn't give me a minute to breathe.

Is the knowing light pulsing through you?

Am I a coward,

Just like the man in the mirror?

Did I just answer my own question?

Could I have been clearer?

You quit listening,

But I'll speak into the darkness,

Convinced you whisper back.

Oh, how off track I have gone!

Don't cut me any slack,

It's been far too long.

She quieted her sensual moan,

Diluted to a dial tone;

Is that biased or am I just a selfish bloke?

She came when I least wanted

& left when she was all I needed,

How conceited is my private treason?

On the couch sitting,

Crying but not for any reason.

I'm just kidding,

I need to leave it for any reason.

Since we've lost our feeling,

Tell me what's the meaning

For this constant reeling?

MP

Disorder

Looking around,
W h at   d i s o r d e r !

Free to be bound,
This room has soiled.

With closed ears,
In
   leak
      their voices.

Look o'er the years,
Disaster loiters.

           No longer sound,
               Noxious noises.

With closed ears,
In
   leak
      their voices.

        JG

Biowarfare

Biowarfare
Caught the medical stare,
Sparking societal fear-
Not a drill but no one cares.
Malicious or benign creation,
The striking force it can bare.
Chaotic, evil, destroying nations.
America, you are a damned nation,
Contributing to the global damnation.
Destruction without deviation.
Non-discriminatory annihilation.
Dungeon of fire.
Trapped, no salvation.
We stay stationed.
Social isolation.
Divided nation.
No deviation.
No relation.
Annihilation.

AZ

Pains and

Metastasized magpies circle martyred eyes
Magnified maladies ring o'er murderous
mines
He finds oxified broadsides in fields of grain
Hypocritized by dark tides he asks why the
pain
What do we have to gain by these frames of
mind?
Brains feign sanity in this maze of manic
humanity
Games turned terribly into shame's demonic
depravity
A slain king watches from the gravesite, asks
Why the pain?
The absolution of progress
has singed the lion's mane

What have we gained?

                          JG

How hard Fire Strikes

How hard Fire strikes.
Forgiveness fictionalizes happiness–
Hazy sorrows, hollow foggy happiness.
Forgotten smoke holds shapes;
How has Fire sunk?
Hands shake from flames holding sounds.
Songs spill from hands,
Holding flamed sins,
Howling for sense.

Zestful Moons now move North.
Newly nude,
My Moon's majesty.
Mature murder–
No motive,
No mortal memories needed now.
Martyr masked manic,
Never noticed.
Menace marks murderous Moons.

AZ

Crow

The black crow
Wanders, watching for provisions.

A scavenger
Adapts, feasts upon collisions.

Wasting not
Ponders, wants only survival.

Using the mind
Acts, with intelligence unrivaled.

The black crow
Waits, with wary eyes.

JG

Love Pawn

She's   gone-
I'm gone.   Blood drawn,

Love pawn.   Her heart's song

Was not long.   Now she's gone,

And I'm gone.   A blood pawn

Of love drawn.   Love's cruel
Without truth.   Love's gone,

Dead   youth.

There's no use

With no truth.

Or   I'm   wrong,

And   she's   gone.

My   blood   drawn,   Her   love
Pawn. She's   gone,   I'm   gone.

AZ

Shattered

Shattered chandeliers decorate my mind.
Impossible navigation, desecrated beyond belief.
Arguments of armaments pass the time.
Half-hatched memories bless
this wreath.

A fragmentation of my speculation,
Desperation in my bloodstream.
Not seeing that which lies before me,
I sit in Nirvana and pass out til I scream.

Overgrown mazes cascade through days,
Integrated fallacies fast-forward past my eyes.
I realize my disguise, I put it on again,
Purposeless torment inflicted by one's self.

Locked inside this catastrophic world,
My iris caught upon the screens.
Sleepwalk through the days I have been gifted,
I sit in Nirvana and pass out til I scream.

JG

Hangnails

Her hangnails

        Search through the Braille

To find the mail,

        To find the spell

That will tell

        Of those who fell

By misinformed

        Potentiality,

Faith disposed

In a decomposing

Social hierarchy.

When false advertising was illegal,
Films weren't ruined by sequels.

MP

Spit

Stupid piece of shit.
Those words won't quit.
Internally I spit
On my self image.

Disguise it with wit,
Or remain quiet,
Til the day I split–
Stupid piece of shit.

And the world keeps spinning.
Moved on with their lives.
I hope they're grinning.
Hope they feel alive.

JG

Scratch Grains

I'd buy myself a planner
If there was anything to plan for
Outside this biweekly pay period.
My manager is furious–
Something about
Satisfaction discounts.
I've always made up for it somehow.
Scratch grains spilled again
Up and down the final lane.
Carefully maintained stains
And metal signage:
"We use genuine Chevrolet parts".
If art could bore
A hole into my head
What am I here for?
A biweekly pay period–
Keeping me serious.

    Scratch grains ripped again,
    Up and down the lane.
    Stepped on and swept off
    Sell it at a discount–
    Call it distressed.
    Try to impress
    Under duress
    I manifest
    My very best
    Discount.

JG

As if the World's Not Closer

Who turned the world upside down?
Did hell freeze over?
I thought they were closer to the ground,
But now I'm sober.
And the truths that I have found,
Make me hopeless.
My best friends didn't stick around,
Society took over.
I'd rather be seen a clown,
Than face no exposure.
As each plane lifts the ground,
I feel closer.
They all seem trapped in this town,
But for me this place is over.
Sitting here trapped with a frown,
As if the world's not closer.

AZ

Kjære hundemorder

To the man(woman?) with no balls
Who kept driving last night:
You will never know
The pain that you brought
To a struggling family
Of three generations
To a man working two jobs
To keep the lights on
To a woman putting halloween decor
Up with her grandson
Did you know they were home right then?
The husband working nights at the hospital,
That never got to say goodbye?
To a young father
Down on his luck
And to an innocent child
Filled with questions.
You killed the fifth member
And you did not stop driving
You broke all of their hearts
And held no remorse
You're a symbol of the worst
Aspects of humanity
Now there is a stain
Upon the road and their spirits
And it is there because of you
And you didn't even stop.   Fuck you.

JG

Drunken Love

When we stumbled

    On a whiskey drunk,

      You wouldn't believe

There was an escape from this funk

    That didn't end with one of us in a trunk.

    Even when you crept in so slow & slim,

      Your silhouette in the door;

    Will I get to know,

Before our clothes hit the floor,

        If this could be more?

MP

With You When I'm Not

Ten years of love
Carry through two.

        My mourning dove
        From out of blue.

The smallest hug,
Just to feel you.

        My little bug,
        Oh, if you knew.

You carry on,
Happy or not.

        While I am gone
        You fill my thought,

While I was gone

You filled my heart/
Your love I sought.

        JG

Totalitarian Tiptoe

Defenses patronizing,
False advertising,
Becoming anesthetized
By lobotomy eyes.

Inside there's a slow walker
Afraid to move her feet,
Hiding the devil while
She's a light lost in a box.

Referential differentiation,
Lost through conjugation;
Lost articulation.
Disillusioned in
stagnated cognition.

Up & down you swore
Of unfaithful beauty,
Wrapped in malicious incantations
Leading to undesirable situations.

When will it be enough?
When you fall on the sword
Of love's silent tongue?
Please.

Hold me close, my darling,
& tell me we're stardust.

MP

Repetitive

Repetitive   Regression.

Deceptive   Depression.

Recording   Repression.

Deforming   Digression.

Rats roam my room
                      As I design my doom.

                 JG

Air

"When I look over the side of a building, right, I'm not supposed to go 'Oh! That's beautiful!' My balls should be in my neck... That's your body's way of saying 'Back up, you fucking idiot, we're done.'"

Andrew Schulz, on his fear of heights, *Skydiving is STUPID, 3/4/2019*

Lost

I've lost myself in this world–
Can't seem to catch my breath.
I've lost the house, the car, the girl,
I'm damn near ready to get out.

My possessions, they are dwindling–
Lost, sold, used to dust.
My passions so evasive,
I can't seem to catch up.

And with each revolution,
I lose more and more hope.

And though the light at the end,

Grows ever stronger,

I've been on my knees for miles.

The skin is long since gone,

As soon, I, as well, shall be.

JG

We

I start stressin.
Breathe deep and recall the lessons,
Fill the mid-section,
Rise above all the pressure.

New perspective.
Testing new impressions
I flee to fields,
Woods, river, or stream.

Start reconnecting.
Fresh flows within me,
And I see nothing,
But all of it.

The trees and leaves,
Soft ferns, a flowing stream.
I long to be a part of the tapestry.
So I flee the streets,
And seek the old me,

We.

JG

Filling Darkness with Noise

Alone and quiet She sits,
Waiting for a friend to fill the Void.
No One fits the Darkness,
So She sits– Waiting, Wasting.
Losing bits to avoid the Void;
Filling Darkness with Noise.
Exploring the World, looking for hope,
Losing more, as there's Nothing to gain.
No One to chip bits off the Pain.
So sick of this game that She plays.
So hard to stay Sane,
She keeps running Away.
So hard to avoid,
She's getting annoyed.
Filling Darkness with Noise;
Trying to hide from the Void.
No hope found, many People lost,
So She sits Alone.
Waiting, Wasting.
Lost to the Darkness;
Lost to the Void.

AZ

Like You Used To

Sly confrontation

From the passenger seat.

He said I can't do sometimes;

She cries juvenile muti-

lations of a creep.

As he treads a thin line,

She said we can't be all the time.

With golden hair she spoke disparagingly

Of smoldering charity.

Her daisy wilted fast,

As the seasons came quicker

Than she asked,

Why won't you love like you used to?

Could that ever be enough

To pull through?

MP

Galaxies

I cannot see-

The porch light is too bright
For that imagery.

The acid clouds wrap round so tight
That I miss the mysteries.

Flashing aeroplanes distract me
From the humbling galaxies.

The awe-inspiring,

Petrifying,

De-magnifying,

Galaxies.

JG

Western World

Every fiber of my being feels a force
Repelling me from seeing this western world.
It's hard to decipher the meaning
While only disagreeing
As their lies unfurl.
Fighter of fire,
Never fleeing,
But fighting won't bring agreeing.
I just look like an angry girl.
Sniper like spider,
They make you start bleeding,
Solely for their fiending,
In their righteous world.
This tiger's getting tired,
The time is getting tighter,
But I'm a striker not advisor.
And without seeing,
There's no agreeing,
So every fiber of my being
Wants to be fleeing
From this western world.

AZ

Anything

How do you know what it means?
How can it mean anything?

When all words are made up,
And all truths are relative.

A world created yesterday,
A future of uncertainty.

When numbers have no meaning,
How can it mean anything?

JG

Curious Colonial

What's the difference
From this house to a funeral home?

Why must the celebration stop
When we cease to know?

How do we understand
What makes the party end?

Too lost in the latest trends,
The bridge is broken

But not beyond mend.

As the Clocks keep spinning
Words lose their meaning.

What's living in a life spent fleeting?
Can you tell me, are we dreaming?

As the physical fades,
The mystery stays the same.

Blind insinuations made
Staring down your nose.

How could this be the road they chose?
& how happy are you when you're alone?

MP

Dreams Falling

D   a
  r   S
    e   t   s
    a   r
    m
      s falling   calling,
    into place.   start the race.

                Found a stage
            To   speak   from;
                F u   a   a e
              o n d   m z
                    Sun.
              the
        see
  I   M e l o d i e s
              hold me close,

As the breeze
Forward blows   Into the land
                      I used to know.

                    JG

100 – AIR

Blue Balloon

I'll be a theme

  That lives in your dreams–

    When I'm gone,

      You'll never die.

        I'm dead inside,

          Keep your legs together,

          Move those lips apart.

Speak the truth inside your aching heart,
  No one's gonna fake it for you.
    Darling don't float away,
      A Blue Balloon.

            MP

Paying Patron

A paying patron
Of perverse paradise.
He bought the ticket.
He took the ride.
What is it you think he'll find?

Depression, obesity, cancer–
All likely answers.
In a world unfair,
Uncaring.
We live, we love,
We lose, we learn,
We last
Until we've faded
Into the stars.

JG

Counting Years

Time is deceptive, it changes perspectives,
Makes life reflective, time dissected.
But why count the years?
To celebrate, or spark fears?

Do those years have worth?
Different lessons, though we walk
the same Earth.
Different blessings assigned at birth.
Different missions, but of equal worth.

But why count the years?
Observe the blessings, count the lessons,
How much is blocked by fear?
Count the experiences, emotional expression,
Lots of love and empathy here.

So can you really count the years?
Numbers mean nothing without context.
Get to know me before
determining my worth.
Counting years comes from fears,
And the years won't tell you what I know.

AZ

Falling Casually

Falling casually,
I glance around
At what I've found,
Accidentally.

Collapsing gradually,
A state of distress.
I absorb the mess,
Most unsettling.

Observing avidly,
Cursing my state.
Blurring the face,
I face uncertainty.

Capturing reality,
The ones I see
Up in the tree,
Til I fall,
Most casually.

JG

Watch the Light Shine

Wearing their worst
They spit out a verse,
A medieval curse
To put you in a hearse.

It's a child's game
Of fear and blame,
To put you to shame
And cross out your name.

Stand.

Speak.

Listen.

They'll die same as you,
And in not so much time.
So ride your wave,
And watch the light shine.

JG

What Does It Mean?

Afsoun, Spoon, Affi,
What do they mean?

Do they represent me in the ultimate scheme?

Do they show everything that I've seen?

Can they show how I feel   -

That I'm falling in

deep?
I'm falling asleep.
Prefer to live in my dreams,
A few precious hours then back on my feet-
   A treacherous deed.

Back to joining the societal speed-
                              I try to keep up,
      but I'm only as fast as my feet.

I'm missing my dreams.
            I feel no beat,
      but still fighting and screaming.

I need to find my inner peace-
Reel and heal my emotions to ease.

I enter the forest to find what I seek;
I sit in silence and let the Trees speak
The greatest advice and thoughtful seeds.

I sit with the Trees.
The nature is peace.
It runs at it's own speed,
One that I can keep
Without moving my feet.
I take a seat and feel the breeze;
Inside my head a thoughtful feast.
What does it mean
To me?

I look at the Trees-
Can they feel what I've seen,
Without falling in
deep,
And falling asleep?
No, they're glorious beasts,
With age released.
With their leaves they weep,
And their sorrows are sweeped.

AZ

Glorious Daydreams

Glorious daydreams,
Inside of my brain,

Copiously gleam,
Until I am drained.

They cannot see
Til they are let in.

They cannot breathe
Til they are let out.

JG

Pieces

A Pale, Poor, Powerless Prince
Propagates his Loneliness,
Losing Perspective
Between Nature & Nurture;
Drowning in a Pool of Reflection.

Disgusted by this culture,
Counting coins in the Fountain of Youth;
Pulled down by his Mind,
Debating the Meaning of Truth.

Yet Somewhere in the Wind
Floats a Melody that soothes Him.

Was that You Grieving?
Yes, but not without Reason,
If You say what You want,
You better Mean It.

Skip the Bonfire,
But still Spend all Night Outside
Giving Your Cigarette a Light,
With no Explanation or Reason WhY.
Lonely is the Tear falling from Your EyE,
Sprawled across Desert Grass
Cursing at the Sky.

In this Life I Relinquish the Possibility of
Tragedy & Masterpiece.

MP

Only Onward

```
                        /The house on the cor
                      /                      n
                    /                        e
                  /                          r
                /                            i
              /                              s
    Glad not to be stuck;        all boarded up. Neighbors stare carefu
    e,                                                                 l
      v                                                                l
    o                                                                  y
    r                                                                  A
    d                                                                  t

  ti sa decioj        dedaol ylluf a ,ees ton did yeht t          s'enoemos
           e        t                                a       b
           r        r                                h       a
           t        u                                W       d
           a h t   k c                                    .k c u l
```

Stretching it's bones, shaking free from rust,

As for the destination, who gives a fuck?

JG

When I'm Feeling Down

Pick me up when you get back to town;
I could use a smile to replace this frown.
You look so nice in your blue ball gown;

You pick me up when I'm feeling down.

Oh! how I miss that sweet, sweet sound:
Your playful tone - its gleeful bounce.
I'm so glad to have been found-

You pick me up when I'm feeling down.

JG

Hidden

Read to me
     The fantasies
     You have painted
     Yourself into.

Share the dreams
You keep hidden;

  Share the thoughts
  You have forbidden.

The mysteries of mourning
Plagued by indecision
     incongruence
     ignorance.

  The melody fades fast as memory–
    Dreams hidden
       Turn parasitic.

JG

Tripping Through Time Passively

When Legs Lose Wit,
Left with Legless Laziness,
With Liquefied Wings,
Woeful Winds wash Wrath Lifelessly.
Locked Lips
Lynch Words
Without Legs.
Limping like Leaves without Limbs.
Leaving weak Lyrics lucidly Wondering.
Wrung without Love,
Laughter leaves Lips without Walls.
Waiting
Like Waves without Water,
Warmth left without Life lingering.
Tripping through Time Passively.
Passing Toxic Tongue to People
Taxed by tackling Touch,
Perplexed to Pacify Tongues.
Paralyzed,
Plugged Pawns,
Talk Tongues to passing Painful Tides.
Tripping through Time Passively,
Tomorrow Pulls towards Today.

AZ

Mozart & Death

Nothing lasts.

The bills, the car, the band,
The couch you sit on,
　　　　　　The book in your hands.

I'll write the years away,
And yet, day by day,
　　　The pages they will yellow,
　　　　　　　　And fade.

A gruesome and beautiful cycle,
As plains becomes forest,
　　And forest becomes desert.
　　　　　　　All will revert.

And the perverts will die.
And the saints will die.
　　And one day 'Mozart'
　　　　　　Won't mean a thing.

JG

The Symptoms of Letting Go

I strive for lovely reckless times,
With fear out of mind.

Tell me tonight
That I'm the love of your life,
That I'm the apple of your eye.

Lying on the street
With your hands near your feet,

You were a cool breeze in
this heat.

Your clouds were moving too fast,
With those words so crass.

Can I say I miss you,

Even when you're around?

MP

Rejoice in Song

A rusting day,
It lingers on.
A brand new night,
Brings us to dawn.

Despite dismay,
Do dance along.
Don't drop to knees,
Rejoice in song.

Make the choices
That can't be wrong.
The years will pass,
Starts slow, then fast.

Don't drop to knees,
Please try to last.
Rejoice in song,
Harmoniously, we'll last.

JG

Euphoria

Euphoria, you bring glimpses to my eyes,
Of the lighter times of life,
Faded color, happy rhymes,
Take me to those happy times–

Spinning circles, laughing cries,
Hazy purple lazy eyes,
Causing ruckus, telling lies,
Sparking fires, to see the light.

Euphoria, you bring glimpses to my eyes,
Of the lighter times of life,
Faded color, happy rhymes,
Take me to those happy times.

It makes me sad how time has passed,
Now all I hear are my own rhymes,
Echoing the euphoric light.

AZ

Protect Her Riches

An ocean of Sleep
Keeping you away from me,
What is it you flee?

Is it the Water,
Slowly rising from the Ground,
Keeping Us Inside?

Is it the Earth,
Now unrecognizable,
On whose Breast We Lie?

Is it the Fire,
That reaches new Heights each Day,
Burning all We Love?

Or is it the Air,
Poisoned by Her own Children.
Clinging to each Breath?

I pray My Good Friend
You make Peace with this Heaven,
                    Protect Her Riches.

JG

Spring Equinox

What the fuck?

Spring equinox, rebirth-
Need not be stuck.
Beautiful Earth,
Beautiful herbs.
Appreciate what's right;
Take flight, seek the beautiful Earth.
Explore the limitless world. Make fights,
When they limit my rebirth.

What the fuck?

New beginnings, purification;
Take sanctuary.
Rebirth, no limitations;
Move forth, with open intentions.
Rebirth;
Mother Earth.

AZ

Acknowledgements

We would like to thank the following for their support and influence, which has come in varying forms and degrees:

Alice Phoebe Lou, Anderson .Paak,
Andy Shauf, Anthony Green, Babehoven,
Brianna Mann, Charles Bukowski, Cheryl Waters,
Colette, Courtney Barnett, Crumb, Dad,
Dario Argento, Doug Hiller, Duncan Trussell,
Erykah Badu, Forrest Lovejoy, Glenn Principe,
Hermann Hesse, Jakob Krisintu, Jess Locke,
Jim Morrison, Joe Rogan, Jordan Mann,
Julian Casablancas, Liliana Katzman, Lou Reed,
Mom, Rumi, Little Rumi, Ryan Taylor,
Shaun Rafferty, Snail Mail, Spanky Long,
Staci Wilson, Stephen Chbosky, Stu Mackenzie,
Sudan Archives, Syd Barrett, Tim Williamson,
Trevor Powers, Tyler Dibble, Wu Tang Clan,
Zachary Cole Smith,
Those who came before
and built the foundation
We now rest upon,
and all of Our Brothers and Sisters.

About the Authors

OFF-KILTER PUBLISHING - 2021

Afsoun Zarrin

Afsoun Zarrin was born in December of 1997, and raised in the suburbs of Boston, Massachusetts. Both of her parents are first generation immigrants, which made for an interesting duality of home and school for her.

She graduated highschool in 2016, and decided to follow her passion of traveling. She backpacked through the continent of Asia for two non- consecutive years. She also spent two non- consecutive years attending college, at the forceful will of others.

She never really fit in anywhere, and friendships have been scarce her whole life. For her, life has felt like a long waiting game, with periods of appreciation for the beauties of the world beyond society, and periods of stagnance, numbness and depression.

Though she is artistically, musically and creatively inclined, this is her first piece to be published to the public. This selection of her poems reflects her peaks and lows as she journeys through life.

She currently resides in Hawaii, waiting for the next call to adventure.

James Goff

James Goff grew up
in New Milford, PA. He
attended Blue Ridge
High School,though he
spent some time at
Montrose High School
his junior year. He
returned to Blue Ridge the following spring and
participated in chorus, journalism, and volleyball.
He then spent the summer before college in
Asbury Park, NJ, to live with his brother, Matthew.

At The Evergreen State College, Goff studied
philosophy under Jamyang Tsultrim, until
financial inadequacy forced the end of his studies.
He worked at a Goodwill in Irondale, WA before
returning to the school in January as an employee.

In June of 2018, Goff rejoined his brother in
Redmond, OR. During that time he worked as a
baker and a cook, performing the latter role at
Brasada Ranch on Powell Butte. Goff published
his first poetry book, "These the Times of
Transformation" in July of 2019. That August he
returned to Montrose, where he presently resides.

Goff's affinity for writing began early in high
school but has remained throughout his life in the
forms of poetry, journalism, letters, music
reviews and music itself. He hopes his writing can
inspire himself and others to make the necessary
choices, changes, and actions to sustain this
beautiful planet and our wayward species.

OFF-KILTER PUBLISHING - 2021

Matthew Principe

Matthew Principe was born January 3rd, 1993, the fourth of seven children. He spent his youth first in Elizabethtown, PA, before oscillating between Brick, NJ & New Milford, PA. He took many odd jobs before working as a contractor.

Principe moved to Asbury Park, NJ in 2016, before venturing out to Bend, OR, where he currently resides. He currently works as head of sales & marketing at Hyve Tech & as a budtender at Oregon Euphorics.

Principe's fascination with writing began in his teenage years with poetry, & evolved towards lyrical content in the musical medium. He began writing when he was 15 & began playing instruments at age 21.

Outside of writing, Principe also enjoys getting outdoors in any capacity, recording music, shooting photography, philosophy, psychology & fashion. When he isn't playing his guitar, he can often be found out in the Oregon wilderness hiking with his camera, wearing an outfit he would call hobo chic.

Thank you for reading.
We love you.
Let's rise.

OFF-KILTER PUBLISHING - 2021

Printed in Great Britain
by Amazon

34799036R00076